Did Jesus Give Me Power

ACKNOWLEDGEMENT

I Would Like To Acknowledge
Jesus Christ
As My Lord And Savior
I Acknowledge God As The
CREATOR OF HEAVEN AND EARTH
I Thank God For All That He Has Given Me
I Thank
God
For All My Talents and Gifts.
I Recognize That The Lord Gave Me This Gift,
Which Allows Me To Share With Children
And
Everyone That Participates In The Reading
Of The Literary Material That I Produce
Through The Commission Of God.

Thank You
Lord God
I Will Forever Be Grateful
For Your Trust In Me

Pamela Denise Brown

2

BOOKS SPEAK
B
FOR YOU

To All Children
Loving You All
I Am.
Inspiring You To Love God
As He Loves You
Through The Inspiration
Of My Books.

REMEMBER
WORDS
ARE POWERFUL

Pamela Denise Brown
Goodwill Ambassador
For The Positive Cultivation
Of Children
Author-Publisher-Illustrator-Editor

Books Speak For You books may be ordered by
contacting:
Books Speak For You At
Booksspeakforyou.com
OR
Amazon

The views expressed in this work are solely those
of the author.
Any illustration provided by iStock and such
images are being used for illustrative purposes.
Certain stock imagery © iStock.
ISBN: 978-1-64050-046-4
Library of Congress Control Number: 2017907411
Printed in the United States Of America

A Little Information About The Author

My Christian Books Are Designed To Encourage, Enlighten, Strengthen And Cause Children To Have A Closer Relationship With God And To Also Understand The Power Of Words.

I Create Christian Smart Books For Kids To Inspire, Illuminate, Educate, Empower, Uplift, Develop, Cultivate, Convert, Edify, Guide, Disclose AND Make Known The POWER Of God.

I Also Write Books To Educate Children, To Transform The Way A Child Thinks, To Better Children So They Can Become Successful People. I Write Books To Help Children Develop And Grow Psychologically.

As An Ambassador For The Cultivation Of Children, I Am A Trusted Source Moving To Inspire Children With Ideas That Create Advancement By Urging Children To Open Up To New Ways Of Thinking In How They Deal With Others And Differences.

I Present Children With An Opportunity To Replicate The Ideas From The Pages Of The Encouraging Literature I Produce, Thereby Shaping The Lives Of Children From Any Background, Community, Age, Ethnicity And Gender.

DEDICATION

I Dedicate
This Book
And
All Of My Children's Books
To My Children
Carrayah, Gabriel & Carrynn
AND
Every Child
Around The World

Did Jesus Give Me Power

I Feel

Strong

What Does It Mean To Be
Strong?

_____

_____

I

Feel

Confident

What Does It Mean To Be

Confident?

_____

_____

I
Feel
Sure

What Does It Mean To Be
Sure?

_____

_____

I

Feel

Empowered

What Does It Mean To Be

Empowered?

_____

_____

I

Feel

Certain

What Does It Mean To Be

Certain?

_____

_____

I
Feel
Secure

What Does It Mean To Be
Secure?

_____

_____

I

Feel

Optimistic

What Does It Mean To Be

Optimistic?

_____

_____

I
Feel
Solid

What Does It Mean To Be Solid?

_____

_____

I
Feel
Energized

What Does It Mean To Be Energized?

_____

_____

I
Feel
Settled

What Does It Mean To Be Settled?

_____

_____

I

Feel

Unstoppable

What Does It Mean To Be
Unstoppable?

_____

_____

I
Feel
Positive

What Does It Mean To Be Positive?

_____

_____

Absolute

And

Certain

Too

Did Jesus
Give Me
Power
Mommy I'm
Asking You

Spanish

¿Jesús
Dame
Poder
Siento
Fuerte
yo
Sensación
Confidente

yo
Sensación
Por supuesto

yo
Sensación
Empowered

yo
Sensación
Cierto

yo
Sensación
Seguro

yo
Sensación
Optimista

yo
Sensación
Sólido

yo
Sensación
Energizado

yo
Sensación
Colocado

yo
Sensación
Imparable

yo
Sensación
Positivo

Absoluto
Y
Cierto
También

¿Jesús
Dame
Poder mamá que te estoy
preguntando

Coloring Pages

SALVATION

TRUTH

RIGHTEOUSNESS

PEACE

GOSPEL

WORD of GOD

FAITH

I can do all things through CHRIST who strengthens me

Philippians 4:13

ASK AND IT WILL BE GIVEN TO YOU; SEEK AND YOU WILL FIND; KNOCK AND THE DOOR WILL BE OPENED TO YOU.

matthew 7:7

Bible Questions

(Circle The Correct Answer)

1. Who Died For Your Sins?

   a. Jesus

   b. Adam

2. How Do You Get To Heaven?

   a. Living Right

   b. Accepting Jesus And Believing In Him

3. How Many Days Did Jesus Fast In The Wilderness?

a. 97

b. 40

4. How Many Commandments Did God Give Moses To Write?

a. 17

b. 10

5. What Was The Name Of The Virgin That Birthed Jesus?

a. Sarah

b. Mary

6. How Many Disciples Did Jesus Have?

    a. 13

    b. 12

7. How Many Books Are There In The Bible?

    a. 33

    b. 66

8. Who Did Jesus Raise From The Dead?

    a. Lazarus

    b. Steven

9. Who Betrayed Jesus?
   a. Jeremiah
   b. Judas

10. What Did God Create On The Sixth Day?
    a. People
    b. Animals

11. Who Did God Tell To Build An Ark?
    a. Job
    b. Noah

12. What Was Simon Peter Before
    He Became A Apostle?
    a. Farmer
    b. Fisherman

13. What Name Is Paul Known By
    Before He Begins His
    Missionary Journey?
    a. Timothy
    b. Saul

14. How Does Judas Signal Jesus's
    Identity To The Roman
    Officials?
    a. With A Handshake
    b. With A Kiss

15. How Many Tribes Did Israel Have?

a. 31

b. 12

16. What Language Is Most Of The New Testament Given In?

a. Hebrew

b. Greek

17. What Was The Last Gospel Written?

a. Mark

b. John

18. What Is The Name Of The
    Second Book In The Bible?
    a. Leviticus
    b. Exodus

19. How Many Brothers Did
    Joseph Have?
    a. 15
    b. 11

20. What Was The First Miracle
    Jesus Performed That Was
    Recorded In The Bible?
    a. Raising The Dead
    b. Turning Water Into Wine

21. What Was The Name Of
Joseph's Baby Brother?
a. Simon
b. Benjamin

22. What Was The Name Of The
Mountain Where Moses Was
Given The 10 Commandments?
a. Mt. Sinai
b. Mt. Rushmore

23. Who Did Boaz Marry?
a. Mary
b. Ruth

24. What Was The Name Of The Nephew That Traveled With Abraham?

a. Job

b. Malachi

25. Who Were Cain And Abels Parents?

a. Sarah And Abraham

b. Adam And Eve

26. Who Found Moses In The River As A Baby?

a. Pharaoh

b. Pharaoh's Daughter

27. What Did Solomon The King
    Ask God To Give Him?
    a. Money
    b. Wisdom

28. What City Was Jesus Born In?
    a. Ethiopia
    b. Bethlehem

29. What Type Of Insect Did
    John The Baptist Eat In The
    Desert?
    a. Grasshoppers
    b. Locusts

30. Who Recognized Jesus As The Messiah When He was Presented At The Temple As A Baby?
a. Simeon
b. Joseph

WORD SEARCH

R	H	H	T	I	A	F
J	E	S	U	S	U	N
F	A	M	I	L	Y	K
Z	V	B	H	D	J	H
C	E	V	O	L	M	A
F	N	T	P	G	Q	T
O	B	P	E	A	C	E

Find These Words

1. Jesus
2. Love
3. Family
4. Peace

5. Hope
6. Faith
7. Heaven

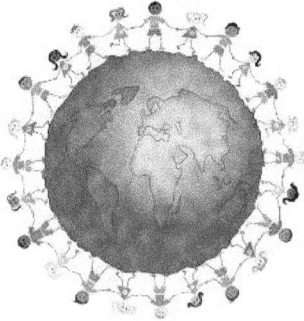

A Special Dedication
To All The Children Around The World

- Afghanistan
- Albania
- Algeria
- Andorra
- Angola
- Antigua and Barbuda
- Argentina
- Armenia
- Australia
- Austria
- Azerbaijan
- B

- Bahamas
- Bahrain
- Bangladesh
- Barbados
- Belarus
- Belgium
- Belize
- Benin
- Bhutan
- Bolivia
- Bosnia and Herzegovina
- Botswana

- Brazil
- Brunei
- Bulgaria
- Burkina Faso
- Burundi
- C
- Cabo Verde
- Cambodia
- Cameroon
- Canada
- Central African Republic (CAR)
- Chad
- Chile
- China
- Colombia
- Comoros
- Democratic Republic of the Congo
- Republic of the Congo
- Costa Rica
- Cote d'Ivoire
- Croatia
- Cuba
- Cyprus
- Czech Republic
- D
- Denmark
- Djibouti
- Dominica
- Dominican Republic
- E
- Ecuador
- Egypt
- El Salvador
- Equatorial Guinea
- Eritrea
- Estonia

- Ethiopia
- F
- Fiji
- Finland
- France
- G
- Gabon
- Gambia
- Georgia
- Germany
- Ghana
- Greece
- Grenada
- Guatemala
- Guinea
- Guinea-Bissau
- Guyana

- H
- Haiti
- Honduras
- Hungary
- I
- Iceland
- India
- Indonesia
- Iran
- Iraq
- Ireland
- Israel
- Italy
- J
- Jamaica
- Japan
- Jordan
- K
- Kazakhstan
- Kenya
- Kiribati
- Kosovo
- Kuwait
- Kyrgyzstan
- L
- Laos
- Latvia
- Lebanon

- Lesotho
- Liberia
- Libya
- Liechtenstein
- Lithuania
- Luxembourg
- M
- Macedonia
- Madagascar
- Malawi
- Malaysia
- Maldives
- Mali
- Malta
- Marshall Islands
- Mauritania
- Mauritius
- Mexico
- Micronesia
- Moldova
- Monaco
- Mongolia
- Montenegro
- Morocco
- Mozambique
- Myanmar (Burma)
- N
- Namibia
- Nauru
- Nepal
- Netherlands
- New Zealand
- Nicaragua
- Niger
- Nigeria
- North Korea
- Norway
- O
- Oman
- P
- Pakistan
- Palau
- Palestine
- Panama

- Papua New Guinea
- Paraguay
- Peru
- Philippines
- Poland
- Portugal

- Q
- Qatar
- R
- Romania
- Russia
- Rwanda
- S
- St. Kitts and Nevis
- St. Lucia
- St. Vincent and the Grenadines
- Samoa
- San Marino
- Sao Tome and Principe
- Saudi Arabia
- Senegal
- Serbia
- Seychelles
- Sierra Leone
- Singapore
- Slovakia
- Slovenia
- Solomon Islands
- Somalia
- South Africa
- South Korea
- South Sudan
- Spain
- Sri Lanka
- Sudan
- Suriname
- Swaziland
- Sweden
- Switzerland

- Syria
- T
- Taiwan
- Tajikistan
- Tanzania
- Thailand
- Timor-Leste
- Togo
- Tonga
- Trinidad and Tobago
- Tunisia
- Turkey
- Turkmenistan
- Tuvalu
- U
- Uganda
- Ukraine
- United Arab Emirates (UAE)
- United Kingdom (UK)
- United States of America (USA)
- Uruguay
- Uzbekistan
- V
- Vanuatu
- Vatican City (Holy See)
- Venezuela
- Vietnam
- Y
- Yemen
- Z
- Zambia
- Zimbabwe

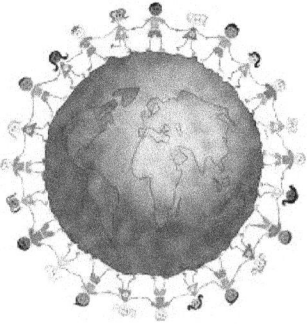

ANOTHER SPECIAL DEDICATION TO
ALL THE CHILDREN WITH LOVE
IN CITIES IN THE
UNITED STATES OF AMERICA

Albany, NY	Baltimore, MD
Albuquerque, NM	Baton Rouge, LA
Anchorage, AK	Billings, MT
Annapolis, MD	Biloxi, MS
Atlanta, GA	Bismarck, ND
Atlantic City, NJ	Bloomsburg, PA
Augusta, ME	Boise, ID
Austin, TX	Boston, MA
Bakersfield, CA	Buffalo, NY

Burlington, VT
Carson City, NV
Charleston, SC
Charleston, WV
Charlotte, NC
Charlottesville, VA
Cheyenne, WY
Chicago, IL
Chicago, IL
Cleveland, OH
Colorado Springs, CO
Columbia, SC
Columbus, OH
Concord, CA
Concord, NH
Corpus Christi, TX
Dallas, TX
Davenport, IA
Daytona, FL
Denver, CO
Des Moines, IA
Des Plaines, IL

Detroit, MI
Dover, DE
Durham, NC
Erie, PA
Eugene, OR
Fayetteville, NC
Flagstaff, AZ
Frankfort, KY
Ft. Lauderdale, FL
Gettysburg, PA
Greenville, SC
Hampton Roads, VA
Harrisburg, PA
Hartford, CT
Helena, MT
Hollywood, CA
Honolulu, HI
Houston, TX
Huntsville, AL
Indianapolis, IN
Jackson, MS

Jackson Hole-
Grand Tetons, WY
Jacksonville, FL
Jefferson City,
MO
Jim Thorpe, PA
Juneau, AK
Kansas City, MO
Knoxville, TN
Lake Tahoe, NV
Lancaster, PA
Lancaster /
Central PA
Lansing, MI
Las Vegas, NV
Las Vegas, NV
Lexington, KY
Lincoln, NE
Little Rock, AR
Long Island, NY
Los Angeles, CA
Los Angeles, CA
Louisville, KY

Madison, WI
Manchester, NH
Maryville, TN
Memphis, TN
Miami, FL
Miami, FL
Milwaukee, WI
Minneapolis, MN
Mobile, AL
Montgomery, AL
Montpelier, VT
Morrison, IL
Nashville, TN
New Haven, CT
New Orleans, LA
New York: Bronx
New York:
Brooklyn
New York:
Manhattan
New York: Queens
New York City
Newark, NJ

Niagara Falls, NY

Northville, MI

Oklahoma City, OK

Orlando, FL

Olympia, WA

Omaha, NE

Orange County, CA

Palm Springs, CA

Pensacola, FL

Philadelphia, PA

Phoenix, AZ

Pierre, SD

Pittsburgh, PA

Portland, ME

Portland, OR

Providence, RI

Pueblo, CO

Raleigh, NC

Rapid City, SD

Reno, NV

Richmond, VA

Sacramento, CA

Salt Lake City, UT

San Diego, CA

San Francisco, CA

Santa Cruz, CA

Santa Fe, NM

Scranton, PA

Seattle, WA

Sedona, AZ

Shreveport, LA

Silicon Valley, CA

Springfield, IL

St. Joseph, MO

St. Paul, MN

St. Louis, MO

State College, PA

SurfScranton, PA

Syracuse, NY

Tacoma, WA

Tallahassee, FL

Tampa, FL

Topeka, KS

Trenton, NJ

Tulsa, OK

Tuscon, AZ

Tyler, TX
Washington, DC
Wichita, KS
Wilkes-Barre, PA
Williamsburg, VA
Williamsport, PA
Wilmington, DE
Yuma, AZ

THE BOOKS
700 BOOKS IN 60 DAYS

I was commissioned by God to first write
40 books in 40 days, which I completed
June 2015,
Then commissioned again by God to write
100 books in 100 days
On October 1, 2015, which I completed
January 8, 2016.
Commissioned Again June 7, 2016 to write
700 books in 60 days starting in July, 2016,
IF YOU ARE READING THIS IT MEANS I
COMPLETED THEM

Thank You

For Purchasing This Book.
In Your Purchase, You Are
Celebrating With Me, The
Completion Of One Of God's Many
Works Through Me.

This Book Represents, The
Completion Of Writing Several
Hundred Children's Books In 60
Days. 100 Of Which, Are Written
In 5 Different Languages

Contact Information

Publisher: Books Speak For You
Website: Booksspeakforyou.com
1-800-757-0598
Email: Booksspeakforyou@yahoo.com

To Schedule School Visits Or Learning
Centers By Author For Conversation And
Cup Cakes, Contact
Author: Pamela Denise Brown
267-318-8933

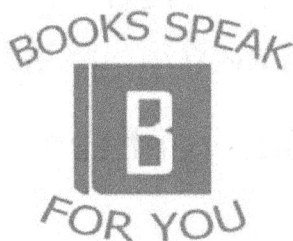

BOOKS SPEAK
FOR YOU

PLEASE VISIT

PDBExpressions.com For Inspirational T-Shirts That Encourages Others While YOU Wear Them. Also Check Out The Coffee Mugs And Games

For More Encouragement

Visit The Group

Pamela In The Light On Facebook For Inspiring, Encouraging Messages From God

www.ingramcontent.com/pod-product-compliance
Lightning Source LLC
Chambersburg PA
CBHW071736020426
42331CB00008B/2052